THIS GREEN LIFE

NEW AND SELECTED POEMS BY
LYN COFFIN

Transcendent Zero Press
Houston, Texas

Copyright © 2017 Lyn Coffin.

PUBLISHED BY TRANSCENDENT ZERO PRESS
www.transcendentzeropress.org

All rights reserved. No part or parts of this book may be reproduced in any format, except for portions used in reviews, without the expressed written consent from the author or from the publisher.

ISBN-13: 978-0-9962704-9-6

ISBN-10: 0-9962704-9-3

Printed in the United States of America

Library of Congress Control Number: 2016959565

Cover design by Glynn Monroe Irby
Cover image: *Wall #6*, Maria Tarasoff. Taken in El Fuerte Mexico (2009)
Dedication quote taken from: "A Pisan Canto" by Sam Hamill, *A Pisan Canto* (Floating Bridge Press)

FIRST EDITION
Transcendent Zero Press

THIS GREEN LIFE

NEW AND SELECTED POEMS BY
LYN COFFIN

Tbilisi, Georgia
January, 2017

Dear Sam,

It was early in 2014, I think, when I edited *Habitation*. There were queries aplenty, but after reading the second section, I started quoting in my summary comments, as, for example, this from Destination Zero:

"Stained with the salts of desire, a shoreline creature talking fear away, I go on confessing to the water, understanding only that the final sentence is death... a mist falling over the moon, that is the signature of all things, beautiful and empty as the solitary seed syllable of the loon." It's six in the morning but I've been up since four- What a gift it is to read these poems, to read <u>you</u>. I bring to bear the analytical knife and find little for the cutting. And learn in the interim of McGrath and Pound and a whole crew of Chinese and Japanese poets and towns in Spain and salal and beeping nighthawks and whining gulls....

Later:
I don't know why I squabble with you. Perhaps because it is a lot to bear, the beautiful words, the old thoughts living again. So many wonderful poems. I lapse into silence. Once in a while, I find you sentimental. But usually, unwavering. Water. Cold. Clear.... Tomorrow, the last installment. For Esme, with love and squalor. For Sam, with love and gratitude.

Finally:
A real rush at the end- Your wonderful work keeps on giving, even on repeated and suspicious readings. I will send you a real reaction, after I recover. It is amazing that even in my proof-reader mindset, so many of these poems moved me. I found myself doing research-- watching videos of monks who set themselves on fire and reading about fish that disappeared. Your knowledge is extraordinary, and your gift enough (mostly) to contain it, hold it up, spill it out. I bow to you. I kiss you on both grizzled cheeks.

I have committed the unpardonable sin of quoting myself, because thinking of you-- half a world away, in the press of circumstance-- renders me largely unable to say much in the present.

I send you this book as my tribute to your gritty wisdom, your generous integrity.

With all due respect, I love you.

For

Sam Hamill

Palms together: *gassho.*

Other Books by Lyn Coffin

Human Trappings

The Poetry of Wickedness

Crystals of the Unforeseen

East and West

Joseph Brodsky Was Joseph Brodsky

A Marriage Without Consummation

Translations by Lyn Coffin

Elegies by Jiří Orten

The Plague Column by Jaroslav Seifert

Poems of Akhmatova

More than One Life by Miloslava Holubova

Islands in the Stream of Time by Germain Droogenbroodt

Georgian Poetry: Rustaveli to Galaktion

The Knight in the Panther Skin by Shota Rustaveli

Still Life with Snow by Dato Barbakadze
(translated with Nato Alhazishvili)

White Picture by Jiri Orten

Animalarky by Zaza Abiadnidze

TABLE OF CONTENTS

as fitting for poets (or poems) by Dato Barbakadze / 13

HUMAN TRAPPINGS (1980)

FORCE OF ONE / 17
SALMON / 18
BANK OF AMERICA / 19
THE BLACKBIRD TALKS TO THE MUSIC STUDENT / 20
THE THASOS KOUROS / 21
BACK IN THE CLINIC / 22
THE DISH RAN AWAY WITH THE SPOON / 23
INDIAN SUMMER / 24
A LITTLE GIRL'S DRAWING / 25
SOUTH FROM MY MOUTH / 26
AN OLD SNAPSHOT / 27
ROUSSEAU: A MIRROR SONNET / 28
OEDIPUS AND THE SPHINX / 29

THE POETRY OF WICKEDNESS (1981)

FINE DISTINCTIONS / 31
NOW'S THE TIME / 29
THE DEATH OF ALLEN GINSBERG / 34
THE DIME-STORE FISH / 35
CROSSING THE BRIDGE / 36
AN AMERICAN POET GOES ABROAD (circa. 1920) / 37
VICTORIANS IN TIMES OF DROUGHT / 38
IN MEMORY OF ROETHKE / 40
THE ASPEN POEMS / 41
BRODSKY'S MEMORIES OF PRISON / 42
WHEN I WAS CRAZY / 43
RECOGNIZING THE SOUND / 44
THE FOX VITA / 46
A LIFE / 47
THE POETRY OF WICKEDNESS / 48

CRYSTALS OF THE UNFORESEEN (1999)

THE STATION / 50
IT ISN'T LOVE / 52
INTRO TO LIT / 53
ZOMBIE / 55
FEBRUARY / 56
ESCAPE FROM THE LOCKER ROOM / 57
CRYSTALS OF THE UNFORESEEN / 58
PISTOLS AND SILVER POLISH / 59
THE ARMORED GIRL / 60
READING BY THE BRASS LAMP / 61
THE REFRIGERATOR SPEAKS / 62
MILKING THE COW OF MY DREAMS / 63
THE DEER HAREM / 64

EAST AND WEST (2012)

EURYDICE'S MOTIVATION / 66
THE CHAMBER WHERE HEAT IS TRAPPED / 67
DELIVERY / 68
KYNEGEIROS / 69
AN ERASED POEM BY BILLY COLLINS / 70
CEMETERY / 71
A CHILD'S CHRISTMAS IN ATHENS, OHIO / 72

JOSEPH BRODSKY WAS JOSEPH BRODSKY (2012)

NOTHING BUT BLUE (A DOOR THAT DOESN'T EXIST) / 73
BRODSKY REVISITED / 74
A GOOD QUESTION / 75
LATE FALL / 77
HOW GOD SPEAKS TO US / 78
THE RECEPTION LINE / 79
SISTER MARY ALGEBRA / 81
OH / 82

A MARRIAGE WITHOUT CONSUMMATION (2015)

INHERITANCE / 83
LOOK AT THE STARS / 84
THE PATH FROM YOU TO GOD / 85
A PRAYER FOR AUTHORS / 86
A POEM THAT ESCAPED ME / 87
THE OX / 89

NEW AND UNCOLLECTED POEMS

GOODBYE, GODOT / 90
THINGS KEEP TAKING YOU AWAY FROM ME / 92
LIFE WITH ENRIQUE / 93
PARADELLE ON LOVE / 96
A CLEAR GLASS BOWL / 97
WILLIAM OF THE APPLES AND THE ARROW / 98
RODIN'S GIRLFRIEND / 99
A WOMAN OF YEMEN / 101
A MAN OF YEMEN / 103
she moves swiftly / 104
EDGE POEM / 105
NED'S ARIA / 106
RECRUDESENCE / 108
PROTEST POEM / 109
ROXANNE'S ROOM / 110

as is fitting for poets (or poems)

1.

If I wanted to compare Lyn Coffin's poetry to something (meeting with the author of these poems- who describes extreme situations and is a master of comparing extremely painful experiences- makes you feel like comparing without imposing on you), I would not need to go far: these poems are rosy flesh and silver skin fish that come into our view as if in a temporary net, from which they try to break loose. Their extreme existence seems to be doomed because of their constant wanting to escape and their failure to do so. Maybe this is the essence of a poem as an elusive phenomenon. Lyn Coffin's esthetics revolves around this question: her poems seem to get into readers' temporary nets for a single reason: to observe themselves in such an extreme situation and learn at least the following – are they happy to realize the fact that temporary nature of these nets is caused by the multitude of them and the uniqueness of each poem?

2.

Lyn Coffin's poems, seen through this alembic of vision, are autobiographical. They start narrating from the moment they are born; furthermore, they narrate a narrative; from the moment of birth they give themselves to experiencing their life experience. Any spectrograph that tried to fixate such an existence would be doomed to a failure. None of their recordings would be credible because it is impossible to describe a process of moving, not to mention fixating movement. What is possible is narrating it from inside to the outside world. A poem that is moving (swimming) and escapes its readers (hearers); the poem that you can read (see, hear) only when it escapes you. So you are quick enough to see the moment a poem escapes you. That is why such poems have the right not to disappear.

3.

Lyn Coffin's poems are constantly lost in the objects they come across, and they collide with them immediately to blend into their structure and internalize them. That is why, probably, there are so many bruises and dark spots on the bodies of these poems. In the existence of good poems, this knowledge is recorded originally: you cannot get anything from those you meet (Ginsberg, a salmon, Grandma's chickens, Sunday plates, Wilde, red curtains brought from India, etc.). You have to collide with them with the body of your soul (or something like that). You have to be devoted to them, and you should make them believe you are immaterial, so that such an unexpected encounter bears a poetic experience that does not require the poet.

4.

Intermezzo I: Lyn's poems are not written: they are manifested. It is possible to assume that these poems are the primary reality, and Lyn's earthliness is the diary in which the historic manifestation of these poems revives. I think the metaphoric impressionism of Lyn's poems stems from the belief that our daily life is a secondary phenomenon. Of course, I am wrong.

5.

"One of Lyn Coffin's Best Poems" is always a door that does not exist. Though, such a poem cannot be "one of the" as it cannot be "the best:" the other poems will not let this poem be the best not because they want this status for themselves, but because they cannot allow the existence of a status where a door can be left open because it is cold; where a lot of children sing with the voice of rain; where clouds capture storms and throw them out of the room, in which a chair is moving in such a way as if no one ever sat on it; where rains change into mountains which you can ski down and enter the door which opens before our eyes and with those eyes see a surprised pair of other eyes gazing back. Yes, What I am saying is this: this poem is an open door which breaks your heart like a closed door that expects a group of children coming through the window and is worried. I would wish this poem to be translated by seven translators into seven Georgian languages so that one more invisible door could be opened this way and nothing else. "One of the best" is synonymous with the phrase "Waiting for Godot."

6.

Intermezzo II: Lyn's poetry coincides with her daily life. These poems are no different than a daily routine of their author. These poems speak like Lyn speaks; act the way Lyn does. When I am writing these lines I am kind of impatient with respect to time because I share this knowledge with the future and not present. Lyn's poetry and life do not resemble each other like halves of an apple cut in two; Lyn's life and poetry is one apple. No one may have seen this apple. That is why it is red, yellow, green, white and so on at the same time. You cannot display it in the museum. You will not see it in the market. We recognize this kind of fruit whether we have seen it or not. Fortunately this kind of fruit can be eaten. Lyn has never lived a life of a successful American. Nor is she living such a life. That is why her poetry is protected from success. In spite of the fact that Lyn is my friend, anyone who knows Lyn will agree with me on this point.

7.

I said that a certain knowledge is written in them, in poems. A poem is looking for a solution. It wants to remember its existence in a time that did not exist with it. It wishes this. This it wants to know. Whose memory is it then when people kill each other and do it as tenderly and affectionately as poets do when they write a piece of poetry? She, the poet, wants to know this exactly when people and their voices are surrounded by smoke and, untimely, are falling down – from America, Vietnam, Iraq, Africa, Georgia = into another existence. It is impossible to stop these people. Likewise, it is impossible to stop a poem. A poem and the poet want to know this: how is it possible for a poem to be born in God's darkened streets? Doesn't the poet resemble a human hiding in an ambush ready to pull a trigger? Their ultimate question is this: is this a correctly put question? And if this is a wrongly put question, then why (and not how) is it possible that poems cannot stop people's unnatural falling into emptiness? This is what Rodin's girlfriend, Rodin, yoked oxen, and Lyn Coffin want to know. They love this knowledge or this desire. Perhaps, that is why poems like Lyn Coffin writes manifest themselves.

Dato Barbakadze
March 7, 2017
Translated by Zaal Zurabashvili

FORCE OF ONE

In the dream I don't know I'm having,
I'm climbing a box.
On the box is the sentry
you once described,
sleeping his final sleep.
I climb the box.
I plunge
your grandfather's sword in his chest.
Dirty water drains out as if from a sponge,
and he disappears.
I bring my hands to bear on the clasp.
My nails are redder than reality.
My fingers confuse each other, but work:
the clasp unclenches.
Straining, I lift the lid.
Coils of raw piano wire struggle over the side
like parings from metal fruit.
You're twenty-one, wearing camouflage.
You glare at me, your face smudged with coal.
The whole box smolders with the heat of your stare.
Sister, lover, friend and wife, I go to you, I stroke your hair.
I gaze at your blackened face- without fear....
The war is over, I say, kissing you. *It's over and we're here.*

SALMON

without memory
or anything remotely like
an expectation,
with the true sight,
the ungiven gift of blindness,
I thrust myself back and back
back and up and back,
bending and straightening in an arc
like the bow, like the eye of the archer
who sees without sight--
fighting dumbly,
plunging bullet-headed
we move somehow through holes
in provisional nets

exploding upward into silence,
we break unbroken
to the shock of air,
and the answer that we
find and lose
beyond all knowing
is
the paradox:
our silver skin,
our keen and rosy flesh.

BANK OF AMERICA

In Dubuque there's a bank,
an edifice like a squared-off wedding cake,
topped with this classical inscription:
SI QUAERAM (word blotted out by pigeons) CIRCUMSPICE.
Inside, thirteen windows are fed by
a common, roped-off line.
Behind each window, rubber-hatted index fingers
like little red Moseses
command entire seas of green.
Bank officials are full of cerulean suggestions,
and when people talk, the little flares
of their matchstick conversations
light the interior dark
like campfires at Valley Forge.
Carried away by major league ambitions,
some customer in a yellow jacket
lights a cigar. His dreams that night
are full of money-- bushels, bordellos,
plantations of money, money burning
with unusual courage, burning beyond control,
and, in his dream, he hears "Circumspice."
Under his lids, his eyes
are as round as Delphic "O's,"
than which no o's are rounder.

THE BLACKBIRD TALKS TO THE MUSIC STUDENT

"I used to sing at Schubert's parties
 from the tops of chinaberry trees.
 He'd hook the prettiest guest on his arm,
 invite her for an evening stroll.
 That was my cue...
 Of course, with the men, it was different:
 'Kann er was?' the master would mutter, half to himself..."

"Thank you. May I inquire whether you sing?"

"Really? And is it common for you humans
 to like singing, without liking to sing?"

"Curious…."

"No. I'm not so romantic as an emperor or oriole.
 It's just that where I come from, we're all poets..."

"It's not your fault.
 I'm only disappointed in myself.
 You'd think I'd have learned from singing
 never not to sing."

THE THASOS KOUROS

The monumental kouros was sculpted around 600 B.C. A flaw in the marble near the figure's left eye was probably responsible for its having been put, unfinished, between the sides of the outermost wall, to strengthen the city's defenses. It is the only piece of archaic Thassian sculpture to have survived.

Nearly a whole year's work wasted.
The treachery of men or the gods was one thing,
something I almost counted on.
But this- this sudden infidelity of stone!
All those summer months, its marble length
yielded to my hand
in ways no boy, no woman ever could.
And now...
Even the creature Pasiphae spawned
could not have flaunted
a more awful face-
the blind soft look as of someone drowned.
My intended messenger of peace and light
will lie in darkness, bonded to the god of war.
Even the strongest slaves
are sweating as they lower it—
so much ballast for the half-built outer wall,
whose double sureness mocks my own incertitude.
Quickly, I turn away, witness to the burial
of some stranger's child.

BACK IN THE CLINIC

This room is like nothing you ever saw.
The mattress has a distinct tick. It's
like nothing so tacky as a bomb, more
like a metronome, like a parking meter.
We have buried the hatchet, buried
the red flag of surprisingly small violations--
but see these squared-off hands? In white
cones and the corners of uncertain faces
something's being kept on tap
like the faint brown film on the eyes
of china cups. Warnings are posted on slatted
hoardings in the least-constructed places,
the snowiest countries. The sky
acts like a butler opening the door
the length of its chain and the
sun starts bobbing up and down like a
dumb-bunny apple... That's all by way of
saying why
some of us get careful
or forget which way to breathe.

THE DISH RAN AWAY WITH THE SPOON

I've come back to the barn where I started.
Though I rolled door to door in porcelain poses,
I was dry as a bone; now I'm cereal- hearted.
My early designs look like secondhand roses.

Though I rolled door to door in porcelain poses,
Propelled by your stainless steel descriptions,
My early designs look like secondhand roses.
My now-sanguine flowers have Greek inscriptions.

Propelled by your stainless steel descriptions,
I tried to kick the traces and clear the moon.
My now-sanguine flowers have Greek inscriptions,
Yet I played second fiddle in your nursery tune.

I tried to kick the traces and clear the moon.
I forgot cow-eyed nature. I dreamed Pegasus dreams.
Yet I played second-fiddle in your nursery tune.
My fine china life came apart at the seams.

I forgot cow-eyed nature. I dreamed Pegasus dreams.
I was dry as a bone; now I'm cereal-hearted.
My fine china life came apart at the seams.
I've come back to the barn where I started.

INDIAN SUMMER

I curled in my straw-colored chair
on the front porch most of the day--
I was a she-fox in her lair--
slit-eyed, I peered out at the sun,
red, wool-jacketed... Until one
by one the trees let Fall hold sway
and cast their golden, heart-shaped leaves
like so much caution, to the wind.

A LITTLE GIRL'S DRAWING

The house looks like an envelope
someone ought to mail. Its flap
has come unglued and sticks up like
a just-beginning widow's peak.
The sun's a rich-with-iron yolk
that must be eaten before table talk.
The air is crowded with scrawny birds;
between them, the sky's too blue for words.
Some trees are umbrella-ribs, black as crows,
pasted to a ground where nothing grows.
Others are greenish arrow shafts stacked
with five huge arrowheads, piggy-backed.
A serpent has fallen out of the clear
blue sky: no doubt he'll disappear
headfirst down the tongue-red chimney in
a minute... Another lies with his chin
pressed against the base of the wide front stoop--
ready, it seems, to swallow up
the first person who steps outdoors--
a girl, perhaps, who has done her chores.
A pink, forked tongue will slide out like
a tape-measure and then get stuck:
it will turn out to be a "Welcome" mat.
She'll leave her new blue sneakers on it
and proceed. She'll make a home
inside the snake. But not like Jonah's.
Her serpent dwelling is sure to have
a fireplace and comfy chairs.
There's food in the cupboards, cups on the shelf,
and plants in the window taking root.
She has no one to please except herself,
and a girl in a snakeskin is easy to suit.

SOUTH FROM MY MOUTH

I asked him. I said, "Timothy,
this sea... is it of water or of sand?"
And he: "Does it feel wet or dry?"
And I to him: "But, Tim. You know I cannot feel
for real what is outside of me. I
cannot grasp the catching stick, the rasp of dry,
the slick, unlatching slide of wet.
I only get the feeling it's a sea."

He turned back to his carving. Again,
I had to ask, "But, Tim. What's that supposed to be?"
"It's for the sea of sand and/or of water.
Maybe an oar, to part the waves. Maybe a shovel
to dig our graves. To row. To bury.
To ride. To hide. You let me know when you decide."
Sun rained on us. I sought a tree
to turn on me, upset the scenery.

Night came. The blade was done,
Tim laid it out across his knees. His hands
were one with wood. (I don't know how I knew.
There wasn't a moon: I couldn't see.)
Throughout the night I thought, until bright day,
And to my thinking, darkness was a mouth.
"A name by any other rose," it said.
Six words I heard like birds-- all flying south.

AN OLD SNAPSHOT
Acrostic for Chris

Caught in the picture's network of grey cells,
He trails his hand on the sandbox and the
Rude gun of the future clicks empty. I see,
I hear ring-bright stones skip- clip the wave that swells,
Surrendering to this pale shore. The well-knit
Memories leap at me like boys from docking boats.
I elude the sea's green stare and watch the white floats—
Knees, knuckles, were knobs on sturdy limbs. (It
Stays light so long in summer.) On the green lawn
Out back, legs flicked up like rabbit ears, then they
Vanished forever. Pins, needles of light may
Still scatter, but the green-and-white days are gone.
Knowledge has bright pages like the Book of Kells,
Yet we are caught in a network of grey cells.

ROUSSEAU: A MIRROR SONNET

But then I step inside: mirrors surround me:
deep in my timbers, something rat-like gnaws
its way out—I sink in a sea of glass.
Like lampreys with imaginary jaws,
my own vagrant glances nose around me,
check my hulk for spoil. But if each mirror was
a painting by Rousseau, then I'd feel free
and full of animal spirits, <u>because</u>
when I consider his girls, caught napping
decoratively on four-legged couches, when
I see his jungles, his come-again jazz men,
cats intent on scrupulous crouching, I'm released
for a while from my human trappings.
Reverent. Savvy. A serviceable beast.

OEDIPUS AND THE SPHINX

He stopped in mid-stride. Her blue-flame eyes were so
pure they made him recall childhood-- long
days spent with shepherds in the mountains near home.
While the sheep grazed like clouds that had found their legs,
he lay back, amazed that his royal body
could so adapt itself to the common ground.

Now it was all he could do to stand his ground:
her eyes reduced past and future to so
much ash, so much wood to burn. Her body
seemed puzzled together: china-doll face, long
snowy wings, woman's breasts; the trunk, tail and legs
of she-lions. She was keeping him from home--

from the city he'd chosen as his new home.
While he watched, she lowered herself to the ground,
tucked her little-girl face between those hind legs
and sniffed the blood that leaked from her like so
much milk. She licked her soft gray parts a long
time and nosed over the rest of her body.

A sour-milk smell came from her body.
Something-- not fear-- made him sorry he'd left home.
The priests had delivered themselves of a long,
tedious lecture: "Be silent. Stand your ground,"
they'd said. "If you try speaking first, as so
many men have done, she'll sprout two more legs

from her belly and, using those new legs
like arms, strangle you, then tear your body
into small pieces as though it were so
much soft bread. If you want to reach your new home,
wait for her riddle." He stood his ground
until his bad foot seemed on fire from the long

ordeal. The sun was setting and the long
day nearly done when, head snaking from her legs,
she asked the riddle. He sank to the ground
and shouted out the answer. Her body
shaking, she waited for his sword to strike home.
Later, some claimed his answer killed her. Not so.

From the ground, he thrust his long sword home
between her legs. Her body might have survived that. So
he'd poisoned the blade with his father's blood.

FINE DISTINCTIONS
to EHC

You skip past this poem like whatever I can think of that skips--
a stone, a rope, the child of foreign parents
on your light-years way home from parks where giggling bullies
missed you by inches. You've established yourself by now--
you're an evader of bullies, and what they throw
in your direction-- button-eyed bears, milk bottles,
black piano keys that wiggled loose like teeth,
paper airplanes, potato chips borrowed
from tomorrow's picnic, flowers with fancy names.
You skip past this poem, past a man with filmy eyes
and a bed that lowers itself from the side of his room
like a horse that is tired of rearing (or a drawbridge in
the wall of metaphor)-- An empty room, this:
full of dust that swarms with almost instinctual life,
a room where light falls through the window like
an impressionable young lady with strange ideas
of etiquette, caught in a comfortable swoon.
Were he still here, the artist who moved out
would certainly uncork the wine his girlfriend
so foolishly abandoned when she fled,
muttering about men in general, artists
in particular, and holding an orange hankie
like a carrot in front of her own adorable nose.
As it is, the artist's non-detachable hangers
swing their bony hips forlornly in
the closet like-- like a string of hookers
whose pimp's been shot. And his black suitcase, hinges
gone, gapes up at them with an old derelict's
weathered air of semi-phonographic
self-absorption. Now your hand has grazed
the door-knob: the spherical cold doesn't make you stop,
it only makes you stop skipping. Wrapping
one chilled hand in the other like a green
bottle in a waiter's cloth, you proceed with greater
gravity to safer pastures-- down the hall,
first door on the left, across from the bathroom,
the home of the homely English lady of whom
even your mother approves because *She don't keep*
liquor or soft drinks where kids can get at 'em.

Soon I'll follow you down the hall, down the long
corridor. Listen. Don't you hear, in
the bathroom, tap-water running? And,
under that, like river stones-- someone,
(me) seating herself on the rim of
the empty tub as though contemplating
a backward dive onto porcelain?

NOW'S THE TIME

I'm powerless in the face of my own violence.
I have only to see a plate-glass window and my fist
insists on traveling through it in a slow silent film
of blood-- ribbons trekking up my arm,
and with what intricate perversity!
They're trickier, extend a more formal
invitation to return to sources than
bullet-headed salmon pushing upward,
weaving around the small inverted tussocks,
the introjected muzzles, of drinking cows
who, at the slippery advent, raise their heads
afraid to swallow... So there I am, my fist
the latest furniture in a furniture showroom
window. There I am, and now's the time
for you to leave me... Go, friend. Trot past me
up the crowded street, with unlowered head,
sporting a garland on each milky horn.

THE DEATH OF ALLEN GINSBERG

Luckily, the Secret Police came in.
Allen perked right up.
Everybody's glass
was empty so he held aloft a giant wooden pepper-mill
and read aloud the first twelve pages of a verse salute to different kinds
of solidarity he'd just written on the bottom of a Kleenex box.
I felt duty-bound to take the so-called Prefect of Police aside.
"You're not the fuzz at all," I pointed out.
He nudged me with his wing. "Allen would be disappointed if he knew,"
he said. "Besides, we are a force for law and order."
Then they surrounded him (it seemed so damn official!) and wrapped
him in some kind of Indian gauze.
Allen fixed us with his chrysalid eyes and started drifting upward.
From on high, hovering among the Romanesque arches, he spoke:

> WAITRESSES OF THE WORLD,
> KEEP YOUR BALLS ABOUT YOU.

At last he was allowed to disappear.

THE DIME STORE FISH

Do not assume you know what I am or
what happened to me. I was spawned
in a large, colorless world that tasted more
like metal than manna. It soon dawned
on me: the close-knit net of death was my
only out. The time came. I was glad to feel
taken up out of all knowing... I
came to my senses to find heaven was real,
marvelous. I was there! With a few others,
I drifted peacefully through this land
of coral and crystal. But one of my brothers
stiffened, the net came down. I can't understand.
Even here in heaven, it seems, death descends.
What happens to those for whom heaven ends?

CROSSING THE BRIDGE

I stand in grandmother's kitchen and look at the picture
painted on a Sunday plate. At the center
of the stunning Chinese sunshine, the blue wall
on the far hill looks impossibly good, breathtakingly
appropriate. In addition, I see
men with hats like arrowheads, mandarin men,
pushing a red wheelbarrow over the bridge
at the heart of the white-as-an-apple sunshine.
And in the center of that red commotion
is a flicker of chickens, about as many chickens
as grandmother used to keep. Then, across
the blue-veined perfection of that eggshell wall, across
that eastern construct, something extends itself,
comes into its own. I have no doubt it's grandmother's
wisteria. Her trailing Georgia blooms deserve
their place of honor on that arched blue barrier.
The summer evening smoke of their fragrance
establishes sunshine and marching men, colors
that vision of chickens and bridge, and makes it this,
makes it what I see... I stand in grandmother's kitchen,
lost in the picture painted on her Sunday plates.

AN AMERICAN POET GOES ABROAD
circa 1920

New York sits like a three-legged cart at
the corner, heaped with huge apples and hoping
to be enormously upset. Summer here
is a brass reproduction of Whistler's
mom, dead as a lion-flanked door.
No one wants to be one of the flies struggling
in or out of this large red Gogolian
boutonniere? So why don't we simply
let go? "Go and let go," as Jesus
said. Or maybe it was Oscar Wilde.

VICTORIANS IN TIMES OF DROUGHT

In a world of silent pendulums, evening falls.
The central sound is of the boot never dropped.
One hobnailed boot lands upright, thuds
on the narrowest board in the room,
the floorboard running closest to his side of
the bed, a maple four-poster where his parents
obligingly died two years ago, one after the other,
a death as regular as their lives. His thirty-year-old
bride, who has been married to him half her life, lies
rigid and waiting. Standing high over the bed in the
not-quite darkness, he has an over-view of his
domestic geography, seeming to see beneath
the homespun surface of things. The wordless comes to him
in a rush... This quilted bed, this patchwork farm,
their meager swells hide bones and boulders that
begrudge not *him* so much as what he does,
how he requires them to behave.
The shale outcroppings, the muddy waterhole,
fences that threaten to unravel the land,
unravel *him* like thread... But it, she, isn't
strong enough to deny him: day and night,
they toil at each other. So it is now.
His heavy mounting of the stairs has told her
more than she wished to know, has told her
this would happen: his weight, his drunkenness,
his hard, unmindful thrust toward generation.
The square, knotted-leather jacket-buttons
she sent for and sewed on with doubled thread
press against the length of her spine with a ready-made
precision. And everywhere a button presses,
a barb of bone presses back in the only
kind of answer she can make…His jeans are still on,
though unbelted. She thinks she can tell the spot where
his zipper comes apart like train tracks: each rail
riding the incline of each buttock.
She is glad he is this drunk. He is
just something that has to ease itself like
hot weather. But the wet cold boot pressing hard against
her cold dry shin bothers her.... He makes her wear
her dresses short. He wants his friends to see

what good legs she has on her, he says-- Thin, not like
their cow-wives have. It's a good thing for her, he says,
she never let herself go to seed...
It's true enough her legs are thin and straight
and so white they look like they've been dusted with
some kind of powder-- that new fertilizer he bought, maybe.
Once, when she was sitting in the tub, legs and arms
stretched out in front of her, she had the oddest notion:
her skin and herself had somehow been reversed, she thought:
what people saw of her was just what people
shouldn't see, shouldn't want to see-- her limbs, for example,
her legs and arms, were like riverbeds in times
of drought, when wires buzzed alive with heat and
watering holes were eyeless sockets...
And now, of course, thanks to the boot
there would be a public bruise. It would bloom and flourish--
it would turn purple, orange, violet, green--
a strange, hothouse flower would grow, would spread,
would lavish itself on the chalky soil of her skin...
And if her kin came to the house, they would see it,
they would see the bruise he had given her,
the tropical flower their marriage had brought forth.

IN MEMORY OF ROETHKE

The day seemed ready-made as a suit,
the nondescript suit from respectable ranks
a gangster wears when he goes public.
Everything seemed its own monument,
as if at a party the deep voice of a prankster
who hid behind potted palms had said,
"Nobody move, I've got you covered."
The time was poised like the egg of a rooster
on the peak of a roof in a children's riddle.

He made mint juleps in a yellow kitchen
on Bainbridge Island: he noted the map--
put his finger on where he was.
A trick of sighting turned the island into
the small, big-gilled fish it wanted to be, and
it swam off... He ambled back outside,
leaving the juleps to cool in the pantry
while he had a swim... He took his dive,
swam to the children's end--

and the three ladies every poet knows
were there to lift him out of the water,
his face as bland and noncommittal
as the water, as the sky.

THE ASPEN POEMS

Salt

Crystals.
The taste of my skin.
A mouth as wide as oceans,
deep and bitter as anyone's blood.

Desire (for Neil)

All my dreams are
now giraffian-- awkward,
on an imaged plain. Slowly,
it dawns on me. The sun insinuates
itself around my morning's eastern
edge, unfolds itself in oriental fanfare.
My hands behave like chastened nuns.

Milk

Matron of the monotone,
thick as faith and dull as rest.
Moth-like mouths of mindless babes.
Ice-floes swell a blue-veined breast.
Rumpled cows with fabled flanks,
suns of butter, clouds of cream,
copious horns and melted moos--
I'm awake, as up as sky,
but sunk knee-deep in dream.

To Terry

My tongue once flew like tilting birds
over your salty, poignant skin.
Now like a half-crazed fox it flattens itself
against the back of a baffling cave.

BRODSKY'S MEMORIES OF PRISON

The first prison was built around a large
courtyard that they used to stack
Siberian timber: the whole area
was, to use the Americanism,
under-developed, and lumber was its
only resource. We prisoners existed
to cut lumber, but so many of us
(I don't mean to be facetious, just truthful)
were so busy dying, we didn't have
much-   what's the idiom?-   heart for the job.
They conferred and decided upon
a Socialistic Competition. So,
I said. And what if I refuse to enter
the lists? Simple, they said. Then you don't eat.
The morning came as it always does,
even in prison, and we began:
I had a short, rough axe that suited me
and red woolen mittens, a child's mittens
because of my small hands. I worked like--
not like a maniac, as you would say-- like an
automaton. Lunchtime came and went
and still I worked. When it grew too dark to see,
they made me stop. It was more comfortable
for them that way... Another time, another
courtyard, another prison-- Archangelsk,
I think-- we, just off the train, were camping
in the courtyard, doing whatever it is
prisoners mostly do. It isn't waiting,
exactly, though it looks like it. Anyway,
one of us must have gotten too close
to the wire: a guard shot him, climbed down from
his observation tower, turned the man
over as a bureaucrat turns over
a form, a piece of paper-- checked his neck
for signs of life, found none. That would have been
it, except the prisoner's watch caught his
attention. He lifted the watch hand to his
ear, and listened. What he heard must have been
satisfactory, because he took the watch.

WHEN I WAS CRAZY

When I was crazy, a psychiatrist
had me look at drawings to find out what
was wrong with them. He insisted,
so I locked my eyes on each black and white square— but
there was one whose fault I couldn't make myself make out—
a winter landscape where everything fit:
tracks across the snow, the receding back
of a small, dark man, circling birds. I finally quit
looking, admitted I couldn't find a mistake.
The doctor made a large black
mark on his sheet. "There are two errors in that one,"
he said. "You should note, first, that the picture lacks
shadows despite the clean winter day, the sun
low in the sky. Secondly, the man's tracks
start in mid-snow…" I could hardly sit
still: I felt my irregular heart contract
to something like a knot of intricate
daring, that nothing could distress. There,
in the exact spot where others drifted
to cold conclusions, someone had made a start.

RECOGNIZING THE SOUND

The other patients called him Mr. Too Song
Or Tong Soon. I asked about him
"He's a manic depressive," said a patient,
Harold, a manic depressive himself.
Harold said in the "bad old days" before
I arrived, whenever the shrinks in morning session
asked Mr. Soon how he was, he'd say
"Top of the World, Top of the World,"
then immediately rush out of the room,
down the hall, to the bolted-from-the-outside door.
He would stand and pound on the door until
his tiny fists were red, whereupon he would
burst into tears, cry "Comme il faut!" and vanish
into his room. "It wouldn't have been so bad,"
Harold added, "but he has a bad heart. He
was sent here direct from the *real* hospital."
In the lounge before my first morning session,
I asked Mr. Song where he was from. Many
patients had asked that, Harold said, and gotten
no response. But-- "Vietnam," he said right away.
"I come from the country of Vietnam."
In morning session, after he'd said, "Top of
the World," he stole a look at me and stayed in
his seat.... Later that day, Denise arrived.
From then on, I didn't exist for anyone
but Harold. Certainly not for Mr. Soon
or myself. I watched helplessly as
the tiny couple began to revolve around each other
like the figures in the glass dome of a music box.
Now he spoke only to her. He asked her how
she'd gotten where she was. She looked up and down
his five-foot frame with her beautiful, frightened eyes.
"Through the front door," she said in French. He smiled.
"I can see the top of your head," he replied in the same
language. "Your part is very straight." And she
smiled tentatively back. "Made for each other--
tiny, foreign, and probably both of them
filthy rich," Harold said as we followed them
around the garden during exercise hour.

     The wall was too high for either of them
     to see anything but sky on the other
     side, but Mr. Tong said he'd often walked there
"In my former life, comme il faut," and he
     described the scene to her: the East River Drive
     was just beyond the wall. Beyond that was
     a strip of green and a lovely narrow path.
     Then came the wide river itself. She asked
     if the rushing sound she heard was the river.
     And he, who must have known better, who must
     have remembered all the cars, said it was.
     By making a strenuous effort, it was
     possible for each of us to think we
     could keep up our peaceful circling,
     could walk in our walled-in garden forever.
     But when Denise heard on the evening news
     that a hurricane was headed for New York,
     she turned uneasily to Mr. Soon--
"Will it hit the clinic, do you think?"
     He took her tiny hand in his. "Not at all,
     my dear," he told her. "The clinic is private
     property." And perhaps because, as always,
     he spoke to her in French, as always what he
     had to say seemed to me to make perfect sense.
     The next day, Denise was gone-- sucked up
     by what Harold called, "The vacuum cleaner
     of the big outdoors." I went to Mr. Song's room--
     and found him standing next to the bed, staring
     at where the window would have been. "Here we are,"
     I said in English. "Here we are, you and I,
     at the Top of the World." And had the almost satisfaction
     of seeing him rush past me
     into the hall... Seconds later, down the long
     corridor, there came to me as I
     lay on his bed, the sound of a strong
     but muffled beating,
     as of a perfectly normal heart.

THE FOX VITA

Ars longa, vita brevis-- which is why,
quick brown fox that I am, I've skipped
past the farmer's lazy bowser and slipped
into this whitewashed little coop
where the farmer's wife always neatly tucks
five or six of her plump white
chickens like folded papers in an envelope.
Eyes accustomed to the dark, I see three
mouthwatering feathered poems on either side of me.
Memories of fox disturb their sleep.
The ones that survive to dream tonight
will dream of teeth... And I, Mr. Sly,
dependent on a covey of uncertain clucks
too dumb to tell if the eggs they feel
are under or in them... Well, Ars Longa,
etcetera, especially if you happen to be
a roosting toothsome pullet in my vicinity.

A LIFE

That's more like it, I finally heard him say-
    I'd do without the forceps if I could.
As I relaxed, I felt the world give way.

At ten, I slipped out after dark to play.
    Father didn't hit me, though he thought he should.
That's more like it, I finally heard him say.

At twenty, I had a stage lover. I lay
    trembling in his arms in a cardboard wood.
As I relaxed, I felt the world give way.

We married. For ten years, he managed to stay
    faithful. When he erred, I said I understood.
That's more like it, I finally heard him say.

At forty, beds got blanketed with gray.
    I wanted to die gracefully if I could.
As I relaxed, I felt the world give way.

I dream of God, discover I can pray,
    can be obedient for my own good.
That's more like it, I finally hear him say.
As I relax, I feel the world give way.

THE POETRY OF WICKEDNESS
for R.S.

You know that girl who calls herself my friend?
The other night-- so late that her apartment
was quiet as a house-- she tried to talk
me out of you, out of-- which is, if not
the same, more precious-- my knowledge of you.
Pushing books, candles, wine glasses to one side,
she spread out copies of your poems like maps
of the Holy Land. "See this *vine*? This *bird*? This *flower*?"
She tried to point but couldn't allow herself any such
rude gesture: in the end, she simply let
her hands flutter over that strange terrain
like unmanned gliders or enormous butterflies.
From behind square glasses, her gray eyes flared
with unnatural life, like old spoons held
over the fire. Certainly the quick pulse,
the soft in and out of her now girlish mouth
said-- not to me, but to you, the poet
whose spirit pressed so vividly upon her-- "Oh,
if only..." And all the time, remember, we were in
her kitchen, your poems spread out on the breakfast table
like the unwound sheets from which the body
has disappeared, having somehow managed to distill
itself... "Poor dear," I told her, moving closer--
"You, and I, if that matters, are merely pigments,
tiny figments fusing in the poet's redhot
eye." But she clasped her arms to her breast
as if they were children or a martyr's cross, and pressed
herself back against the hard white metal canvas
of her own refrigerator... As for me,
there's no need to tell you what I did then:
I imprisoned one of her fluttering hands
in mine and kissed her, letting her feel
how things stood, how that was-- woman's mouth
against woman's mouth, soft yielding to soft.

Later, I smiled to myself in her bathroom
mirror: such a thin smile that not even
you, I thought, could have looked so wonderfully
wicked... I thought so until the next morning
when I sat at the breakfast table, reading
your poems while she turned over and clung to sleep.
"Such a long thin smile," I read. "Not even you
could have looked so wonderfully wicked."

THE STATION

I know where I'm headed after I arrive—
an empty station where a wind like
the desert sighing drifts in one door and
out the other, and the remains of windows
are glass daggers stuck like teeth in wooden gums...
My fingers fumble their way along cracks in
what were bedroom walls-- moccasined trackers
walking single-file down dry tributaries...
The roof lifts off--a big-bellied hawk--
and bricks, as if dazzled by sudden sunlight,
tumble onto the bed like staggered children.
What lovers were left left long ago, in
the days days counted-- glass beads hung in decades
around necks so slender no words came
anywhere close, so hands made do, covering
that small warm throb with laced fingers, days
when the interlocked rings left on tables
by two wine glasses could be seen as a sign...
I cannot remember what I thought death was-
small birds' erratic wheelings darkening
the sky at dusk? Horses with slick sides
galloping riderless toward the ocean?
But no. Someone shouts numbers penciled on old
phone books-- A stubbled man in a torn jacket
clamps a fiddle under his chin, and pulls
a thin bow across four thin strings-- whereupon
ghosts push back their chairs and square off for a dance,
a naked light bulb does an electric dosey-do,
hanging down from a ceiling where
a thousand holes drilled in rows more regular
than corn aren't enough to sponge up the silence
which swells like dark water under the music's
shivering glissandos. In the yard, ghosts in
knee-pants swing on tires that dangle from the trees
in nooses of knotted clothesline, the black
receivers of abandoned conversations...
And all around the pinprick house, the ceaseless
prairie darkens--an untroubled ocean
of canvas grass stretches in all directions,
farther than the human eye can see...

A sea of parted grass through which they come as one--
pale horse, pale rider-- at an easy lope...
Nothing to stop them and nowhere to turn.

IT ISN'T LOVE

that grabs me smack in
the middle of the night, propels me out of bed,
sends me staggering through a rented house,
drunk with darkness and bad dreams. Love was before,
which means <u>not now</u>, something I wish sadistic
nuns had beaten into me in second grade.
Today's too late to learn the lesson for today.
What I'm discovering, page after page,
is dislike of the actual. No, I want to say,
I take that back. But you can't take
anything back… it's part of the swelling
chorus of adder tongues turning the latest
haven to a darker, darkest hum. Even
in the morning, when I'm confronted by flowers,
they say the same things, only smaller.
My dreams come down to a dying elephant,
chained beside a hole with a trunk too short
to reach the water, and
a Humane Society that doesn't deal with elephants.
I've been educated: I know what the dream means
and I don't like it. I don't like my eyes in the mirror
that are not mine but my sister's,
my Voted Most Likely to Succeed, married
in Life magazine, alcoholic,
Intensive Care, dead sister who, a nurse said,
asked someone else's family if she was dying
and they, not knowing my sister or
the truth, said No. I remember when I fancied
I was depressed and stayed up until
dawns I liked to describe in *Look ma no hand*s
lyrics but these lines, these nights, are
barrel-chested security guards, all thick
wrists and night sticks, joking endlessly in uniforms
about wet dreams and nude mannequins
in Intimate Apparel.

INTRO TO LIT:
for Judith D.

8:00 a.m. – Guest-teaching English at the high
school. A cornered girl, scribbling. I'd asked
the kids to hand in "a line of poetry";
she balled up three pages before she could give
me one— Almost nothing managed to survive
her strict self-censorship: all the words

had been crossed out except the word "words"
which sat in the corner of the page-- high
and dry, like the fruit powders I survive
on in winter, mixed with water. Had I asked
for too much? Had I challenged her to give
me more than she could give? Or was "poetry"

the problem? Had home or school brought "poetry"
to its knees, pounded truth and beauty till "words"
were all that was left? What could I give
this cornered girl to make her see the high
drama of the classroom now? What if I asked
her which "words" she needed to survive?

The class was staring at me. Would they survive
the hour? Would I? A march of "poetry"
began in my brain, led by a masked
priest, chanting Anglo-Saxon words like "thu," words
that were saddled donkeys bringing God's high
purpose to us before local dogs could give

chase. But quoting the old poets might give
these pin-pierced kids the wrong idea. To survive
their silent scrutiny I needed both high
craft and current lingo, a poetry
written in their vernacular-- wolf-words
wrapped in fleece, that trotted to them masked

as clouds with legs, lullaby lambs. I had asked
the class to write lines of poetry, to give
me fuel, but now I needed to take their words,
make of them a poem to help us all survive.
I would prove to them, prove to myself, that high
poetry was <u>now</u>. They were that poetry.

In response to unasked questions, I'd give
them back their words alive— and sound the high
summons of poetry, thought letting beauty survive....

{N.B. That's what happened, but I was the girl,
and the word I wrote on my paper was "truth."
You that are cornered in classrooms— uncrumple
your fists, speak the inside truth. We need to hear
what you need to say, and life, like this poem, is
sometimes not over quite so soon as you think.}

ZOMBIE

My fingers were double-jointed; my hands might
have been put on backward. My zombie's blood, slick
with oil, sometimes caught fire and burned all night.
I spoke in riddles, and was known to mutter
to myself. At meals, I kept pats of butter
cooling on my tongue like lozenges. After
meals, I hid. I lashed asparagus logs
together with string -- rafts for a dry gutter.
I hated zippers, sing-alongs, boys' laughter,
books with underlined words, old ladies with dogs.
If mother kissed me, I had to take a quick,
hard suck of air, but she found me hard to kiss.
I didn't ask for more, didn't whine or cry.
I fought fights I hoped I'd lose. I didn't die.

FEBRUARY
an acrostic

The snowman has crumbled to a giant's glove--
Have I made it to garaged boots and boxes
Of five-cent valentines? Do you love me now?
Me? Do you dream us into bed, young somehow,
And naked? Then what happens? Do your dry
Senses swing open like garden gates? I
Can feel you quicken when I touch you by
Accident, the way I have to. I feel new
Repertoires come into play each time I do.
Lift me up, breathe on my hair and carry me.
I'm five years old, asking you to marry me.

ESCAPE FROM THE LOCKER ROOM

The locker room stinks of cold male sweat and cold
showers. Towels snake out at him from passing hands
or lie coiled on the wet cement floor
like cold-blooded animals. Old jokes pounding
in his ear are surf in someone else's shell.
The coach's hands and heavy-lidded eyes
send messages he doesn't want to decode,
conjure up a Georgia moon, a man
with hairy hands like the coach, who stood for a while
by the blinds in the Happy Hunting Grounds Motel room
as though telegraphing police
hidden in an alley on the other side
of the hot asphalt highway, "The boy
is yours-- Just let me have some fun with him first."
"Snakes are everywhere," he hears, but the coach
is saying something else. "Any of you boys
on drugs?"-- If I catch any of you..."
And *still*... Even the best of boys knows snakes
are everywhere-- behind the coach's lips
and closed doors and under everyone's zippers...
His teammates eye the coach and whisper, "Did you
see his whanger? Did you see his thing?"
And so it's from the locker room he escapes
when the girl in his social studies class
invites him over with what the coach would call
a "sly-boots smile." "Can you come
for dinner?" she asks, her eyes as blue as dreams,
a thin red sash slicing her dress, slicing her body
in two like a surgeon's cut, a magician's
wound. "My parents will be out." And she's as good
as her word-- They're out, all right, and he's in--
in a kitchen that smells of food and women.
And when they lie down on the rug near the heater
that won't work and she says with a smile,
"Let's you and me-- Let's the two of us keep warm,"
he understands. He burns the past behind him.
Without any coaching, he catches on like fire.

CRYSTALS OF THE UNFORESEEN

In the thinning night the stars draw closer--
children around a sickroom, whispering.
Nobody ever knows what will happen.
Even the window's being opened by
a gust of wind was unexpected-- Death
we wait for, but he lands disguised-- some
Odysseus, some minor injury--
delicate as a change in coloration,
a knot hidden like a tiny island
under the untroubled sea of our skin,
a ragged tremolo in our breathing.
Every cut or bandaid, every bone we
gnaw clean during Tuesday dinner
is a thin rubber band around our wrist--
reminding us, so we stop on our way home,
but can't remember whether to get milk
or dog food. No matter how we watch for him,
Death just comes-- We hear a thump on our porch
one night, and in the morning, there he is
like a free subscription, or a messenger
from the king, with one glass slipper we need
to try. And what are birds who slam into
our bayside windows, what are phone calls
in the cutthroat hours, or the miniature
explosions which mark the end of light bulbs,
what are the children we actually
wanted if not crystals of the unforeseen?
So when love, that impecunious stranger
comes banging at our back door on his way
to every back door in the neighborhood,
selling whatever it is he's selling,
looking for whoever's home with their checkbook,
we're ready to spend, more than willing
to buy the latest in magazines or
blenders, hot to give any God a chance.

PISTOLS AND SILVER POLISH
for Sara Mendel

Deliver me from the mouths of babes
and halls that cloister aging scholars.
Thrust me like an overdue letter
in the back of someone's mailbox
somewhere else. Deliver me from disheveled brooms,
chipped beef, chipped glass, the feral satisfactions
of masturbatory lovers, the yawn
of three-dimensional perspective.
Deliver me from unlined legal pads
and balding men with ponytails and dreams
like concertina wire. Deliver me
from Maplewood, New Jersey, and one way streets
named "Sylvia," or "Sybil." Deliver me
from the old, the young, the middle-aged,
the not-quite famous, from tedium and
tyranny and days that crack like eggs
on thin-lipped china kept to prove the presence
of the doting dead. Deliver me from rebukes,
remembrances, sideboard sermons tarnished
with the smell of pistols and silver polish.
Deliver me from memory and her
steaming minions, bearing platters of food
in hands they wipe on dirty aprons.
Deliver me from masons-- Let stones stay stones,
lying where they fall... Deliver me from
that stool-kicker, my face in the mirror....
From self-importance, self-neglect, and from You,
O Lord, I pray that I may be delivered.

THE ARMORED GIRL

Boxes in boxes, dolls within dolls,
seeds in apples implicit with apples...
When I was pregnant, I carried inside me
all the answers to my own questions.
It's like that giving birth to anything.
The proper myth would have to be Athena
springing out of Zeus's head. But what a strange
Caesarian, to have one's mind sliced open
like an apple by Hephaestus' axe.
It must have seemed to Zeus when he first saw
his armored daughter standing there- full-grown, gleaming,
that he'd been tricked into being a mother,
and magic in that whetted axe was all the god
could think of to explain the shining girl.

READING BY THE BRASS LAMP*

Reading dog-eared thrillers on my narrow, straight,
Unmade bed, I'm snailed up. I don't see how I'll
Survive. I heap my pills on a fluted plate
Saved from childhood. It had a blue fawn and doe
Enameled on it, but they wore away
Long ago. I snub my cigarette in a
Lacquered dish my ex-husband bought. Our so-called
Honeymoon. We stayed in Madrid a whole week.
I loathe bullfights. I read by the old-style
Brass lamp I got at a garage sale-- Hauled
Back home, it blew a fuse. I worked all one night
And fixed it partly-- It only works on low?
Reading, I learn the girl was killed by a Greek
Dissident who loved her. I turn out the light.

* Acrostic 1

THE REFRIGERATOR SPEAKS*

Rap me or dare the door-- I've been left scraped clean,
Unfilled. They slapped their medals on my chest, true--
Stuck me with magnets like a ham with cloves--
So? The only real message is the last one--
"Empty Fridge. Leave Nothing here." I crave a new
Light for my vegetable bin. I want newborn
Lettuce to nestle and fear no harm from love,
Hardened cucumbers or callow troops of
Idle celery lawmen. It would be
Best with eggs blooming like white flowers on the
Blue plastic moonscape tray with protective bars,
And two sticks of butter to garage like cars.
Raw meat, frozen, is the start of every poem.
Don't ask why. Just go bring the groceries home.

*Acrostic 2

MILKING THE COW OF MY DREAMS

I'm 12 years old, sick with a fever. My dad went to sleep ages ago, and my sister just gave up trying to take care of me and is probably awake in her room, thinking about how she's going to get married tomorrow. I've fallen asleep in front of a TV that doesn't work, and even asleep I feel stupid because I'm dreaming about a cow who's so white it scares me. Not even my sister was ever so naked. She watches me come toward her as though the field of corn we're in is a country church all lit up except for one dark center aisle down which I struggle, me, the kid sister, purer than any bridegroom or his whispered *Yes*. When I'm near enough, I reach out. I want to touch her, but her eyes grow baleful: some overweight nurse on her lunch break. My left boot makes a mushy noise. Surprise! I'm ankle-deep in an analogy so new it steams. Her tongue extrudes from her mouth like a thick pink slur of toothpaste from the tube our long-ago mother taught us to roll tightly from the bottom, like summer pants. Her black, squared-off nose is my Teddy's, lost in the washing machine that broke right before Mom's funeral. Her ears are damp kitchen towels that go *psst* when my sister puts them on my forehead, towels she won for spelling "bureaucrat" before Betsy Sands. I know what would happen if that tongue were pried-- the tape my sister used to use to check her bust would get torn. She'd be spanked like in the old days and throw stones at me, spider-webbing my glasses, so I try the back door approach. That tail might lash and twitch like willow or birch, but it's the barn rope we swung on from loft to loft-- It's never let us down. I grab hold and it's Eeyore's tail. I tug-- It comes off and with it, a balloon tied by a knotted string, comes a bulging sack that thumps to the ground. I rip the slick thing open with my teeth and nails. I pound the ground in red-handed joy, but the calf is dead. I shove it aside, fall to my knees, tuck in my chin and begin to butt. I nuzzle the warm white source of luck. Muzzle unmuzzled, I guzzle and suck.... I wake up and it's morning. I'm feeling better and the fever's gone but when it gets to the part I don't want it to get to, and my sister starts walking toward me down the aisle, I still embarrass myself by crying. Because, say what you like, three people is a family, but two people is just me and Dad eating TV dinners and struggling for control of the remote.

THE DEER HAREM

Arrows of sunlight spend themselves in the clear
heart of the orchard. Leggy as schoolgirls, deer
nose through the long gray grass looking for windfall
apples, soft and brown, sweet with rot, small
as a child's fists. He makes his approach down rows
of cedar, dappled aisles of larch. Three large does
sidle up to him with mincing steps. He feeds
them bakery rolls, dotted with sesame seeds,
a pouch full of his father's good Bull Durham.
Soon they all seek favor: they are his harem.
Even with the food gone, one doe lingers
at his side, butts him, nibbles his fingers,
tries to bite his hard white palms, grows shy
when he wants to touch her, he doesn't know why.
From far off comes the yap of his father's hounds:
the deer flee him, a Judas, in stiff-legged bounds.
He's alone. The whole unleashed pack starts to swell
into voice: Jinx first, Miss Molly, Jezebel...
The last skeins of snow geese wrangle overhead.
He thinks of his mother. He put her to bed
last night, a wan child in lace: "I'm not feeling
so good." --The sky spills: feathers, lace, white, wheeling.
His father's girlfriend wears jumpsuits, has full lips.
He thinks of them together-- a shiver skips
from nerve to nerve like a skimming stone. It's late.
He has to milk the cows, fix the garden gate.
He turns and starts walking home. The snowy wind
toys with his hair. He has often imagined
what he imagines now: everything will
be as it was before November's chill
breath made stiff white sails of sheets hung out to dry--
Or better... His father's girl friend will say Why
didn't I think of you as a man before?
He'll roll down the blinds, double lock the door,
and nibble the scarlet lipstick from her mouth.
Mute as swans, geese will glide back from the south.
His father will feed the dogs Durham and bread.
His mother will step forth smiling from her bed
and make the whole house hum as she bakes
lattice-crust pies.   --He'll have what it takes

to keep a deer harem safe from harm's way.
Ahead, like a minefield, stretches the day.
He'll watch what he says, be careful how he acts.
Behind him, snow is covering up his tracks.

EURYDICE'S MOTIVATION

The poets, as usual, got it wrong:
what drew her upward wasn't hope, or his bare
fluted melodies, or poetry.
All strong emotions appalled her: she
and her wants had become as simple as
nostalgia. The need to change, the need to be
the same, were fused in her breast to one new
ambition: she longed to see if she could do
an impossible thing and compress
herself into her former shape, to be less
than myth demanded. She went with him, pale
and patient, because she knew they would fail:
she admired the dark magnanimity
of his task. She'd been living underground, where
tragedy was more sentimental than song.
She lent herself to his journey nonetheless:
she went willingly-- in love and hopeless.

THE CHAMBER WHERE HEAT IS TRAPPED
for Derek

Walking hard on a stone beach, both of us
(as we joked) literally around the bend,
we came to where once upon a time a cliff
collapsed-- the wreckage of what had been
a cottage with a view-- and you began
naming what there was to see, recalling
old brands and invalidated functions
with a doer's, a maker's, a lover's
nostalgia, while I stumbled on, hypnotized
by the forked flickering in my mind
of old emotion, cold event. You turned to me.
"This was part of a wood-burning stove," you said. "Here,
at the heart, is the chamber where heat was trapped."
You showed me where smoke had parted company
with itself, becoming as circular and lazy
as recrimination— "Oh, and look,"
you said. "That two-horse Little Giant motor!
I think it could still be hooked up, and made
to run." "Right," I agreed. "If only
the garage, the cottage, and the cliff it stood on
weren't totally gone." You tried to hold me then,
but I had read the writing on a crumbled wall,
and asked again what time your plane would leave.

DELIVERY

Nothing's maler than a male mailman, but my
mailman is a woman femaler than I....
It's not hot. Fall's already poked holes in my
heat bill. Why do I still wait inside for her?

Beautiful in her uniform, behold she
cometh! She unlocks rows of boxes with her
tender key, saving mine for last. As she
fills the open mouths like a mother bird, I
watch her through my plate glass window. I
think *How nurturing, mindful, and sexy she
is!* Tomorrow I'll wait for her outside. I'll
speak to her. I will. We'll fall in love. We'll
get illegally married. I'll read her my
poetry in bed, She'll touch me in ways I--

Wait.... Tomorrow is Sunday, the day she's
unfaithful.... I know. I'll write her a poem! I'll
dedicate this to her and leave it in my
box in an envelope that says, "To My
Favorite Mailwoman." I like the thought of her
delivering my message to herself.

KYNEGEIROS
for Fotios

It was after the battle of Marathon:
the Greeks had chased the Persians
back to their ships: the Persians
were leaving. Greece had won.
But battle madness fell on Kynegeiros:
he went berserk and tried to get into one
of the Persian ships: he grabbed the bulwark
with his right hand. A Persian promptly
cut that off, so Kynegeiros grabbed the bulwark
with his left hand. That was cut off, too. Then Kynegeiros
grabbed the bulwark with his teeth,
and thus he was beheaded. Kynegeiros,
I'm sure, is my progenitor, my source,
and proud of me, now in my fourth divorce.

AN ERASED POEM BY BILLY COLLINS

"It wasn't easy, by any means… I had to work very hard on it… But in the end it really worked. I liked the result. I felt it was a legitimate work of art, created by the technique of erasing."
– Richard Rauschenberg, "An Erased Drawing by De Kooning."

The name of the author is
followed by
heartbreak,
which suddenly becomes you.

Long ago, you kissed names goodbye,
and watched equation pack,
and even now as you memorize order,
something is slipping the address
of the capital of
whatever is you
in some obscure corner.

You can recall
your own way to oblivion where you will join those
who forgot to
rise in the middle of the night.

No wonder the moon seems to have drifted
out of love.

CEMETERY
for Arthur Phinney

you who fought against inspection
have managed to escape us.

the snapshots we had lying on
the lacy dressers of our minds
sink underwater: toothless fish
come to nibble deckled edges.

yet even what's invisible
keeps disappearing
and our adult pockets
are never empty
of childhood stones

we are inadequate
to silence
but this place of codified regret
shows us who we are

all we can and cannot do

A CHILD'S CHRISTMAS IN ATHENS, OHIO

                    Christmas morning.
      A doorway.   A boy stands
       in the doorway.   A leather couch.
    His parents sit   on the couch.
     Under the tree   presents.
    An electric train: cattle car
            oil car   coal car
         caboose.   A switch box.
        A red light.   A red light.
      A figure eight track   lined with landscape:
        two trestle bridges   stacked arrowhead trees
           white elephant hills   white sledded children.
                  A town out of fable
                    cobblestone streets
                    cobblestone shops
         houses with windows   through which
                one might see   tiny tables and chairs
             big tiny families   everyone laughing.
            The boy stands   in the doorway.
       Thank you he says.   Thanks mom and dad
    for the really great train.   His dad takes a sip.
         His mom takes a puff.   The boy stands
              in the doorway.   On the mantel
                    the ship's clock:
                    tsk. tsk. tsk.

NOTHING BUT BLUE (A DOOR THAT DOESN'T EXIST)

Inches beyond your door, a late spring rain
is falling. Always, when I am with you,
it is spring, and raining. I shiver, and see
the red curtains you brought from India move
in the wind. It is cold, but your door
is open. When I am with you, you always
keep the door open, and it is always
cold. The rain on your roof doesn't sound like rain
but a host of kids sing-songing, "Close the door,
they're coming in the window." I'm glad you
don't hear. I'm glad that your clouds can move
across your sky, unburdened by the storms I see
in the gray and fraying clouds. But when I see
you dazzle your canvas with green, I always
want to live in your landscapes. I want to move
through hills that rise like music and fall like rain.
I want to build a barn to match the fields you
paint, but I sit still, staring at a door
which would be white if it existed, a door
that discloses nothing but blue. Your birds see
past the threshold of the visible- Yet you
brush them, too, into corners. And, always,
because it sounds like pounding children, the rain
makes me think I exist at one remove
from everything. I don't know why your fields move
me so much, or why it hurts me that your door
stays open. Or why rain that isn't your rain
frightens me. Or why no one else seems to see
angels swimming in your skies, but I'll always
feel at home in the abandoned landscapes you
create, among the whirling dervish trees you
scatter like baby dragons' teeth. When you move
the chair I sit on to watch you, you always
move it close to the corner, nearer the door,
sandwiching me between my need to see
and my fear of the cold, inquisitive rain.

But when I see you paint, a door in me
always opens. Rain turns the outside world
quicksilver, and I feel no need to move.

BRODSKY REVISITED
for Gia

I write now to please my Gia
with a Brodsky fantasia—
Gia, you are Joseph's fan
he could have no better than.

You know all the Brodsky saga—
that he was for Auden gaga.
Yet I need to make you wary
of some digging in that quarry.

In that old abandoned site,
comes the Irishman by night
praising Brodsky, Auden Yeats—
is there nobody he hates?

I'm not saying he's a thief—
He's just got small cause for grief.
I shared with Joseph, when a lass,
sexier than sex, his class.

I was married, we were friends.
There our story nearly ends.
Soon he left our state behind,
the Michigander state of mind

Years went by. We wrote. Not much.
Eventually, we lost touch.
Then one day, I read he'd died.
I don't even think I cried.

Joseph, you are where we'll be,
postmarked to eternity.
Your smokes are gone, your coffeed curses,
What remains of you is verses.
In my recent dreams, I kiss you.
When I read your poems, I miss you.
And in these, how bright you shine—
In your poetry, you're <u>mine.</u>

A GOOD QUESTION

When she was six, a girl asked her mother
"Mom, what is poetry?" Her mom smiled
and said, "Please eat your breakfast." At twelve,
on the playground, the girls asked again, and
a ten-year-old bully pushed her face in
the sand. At eighteen, she asked a distinguished
church elder: he shoved a Bible at her
and replied- "Do better, my child, at avoiding
damnation." The last time she asked, she was
twenty-four: she asked her husband the night they
were wed-- and when she asked, her poet husband
sighed. He embraced her gently and after
a moment said, "I'll try to say what cannot
be said. I love you so much I don't mind
being foolish... You ask what poetry is—
it is <u>this</u>. It is <u>now</u>. It is <u>us</u>. This warm night,
that moon, this balcony, the scent of flowers
and us in our nakedness-especially our nakedness...
All I say is old news, though, and I long to make love,
to be deep within you, quiet and moving."
He fell silent and she stood on tiptoe
to kiss him and together they left words
behind them like abandoned rafts. Day followed day
in slow, bright parade and the answer to her question
rooted itself and grew within her.
Nine months later, she delivered a son...
When her son was eight, he ran downstairs
one morning and asked while he waited at
the table for breakfast, "Mom, what's poetry?"
She smiled and when he was eating, she told him,
"My son, the slide of milk on your tongue
and the warm crumbling of just-baked bread
in your mouth, that is the taste of poetry. The drumming
of your feet as you run down the stairs, that
is the beat of poetry, and there, outside,
that bird in our garden who coasts over grass,
casting a shadow—she and her twin below—
the two together are poetic thought."
Her son raised his head in the middle of
eating. "But Mommy-- Teacher said poetry

rhymes. Is she wrong?" His mother smiled and told him, "Keep asking good questions. Know that I love you. And please don't talk when your mouth is full."

LATE FALL

In the house of my childhood, the heat made noise,
the furnace churlish as Hamlet's dead father
in the basement. You could see, indirectly,
the heat come on—our splayed out cat
sitting on the grate, licking herself like
a wound. You could smell the heat—an unlaced
Havisham wandering by. You could taste it
as the must-not must of old afternoons,
stale red licorice brought home from some
silent movie where the heroine was a moth
fluttering around the hero's lamp.
The heat in our house sometimes plucked one's sleeve
like a persistent child.... And yet, if I were
back in that house, and the sensible heat
was turned sensibly on, knowing my family,
we'd all still be cold.

HOW GOD SPEAKS TO US

God speaks to us in schoolmasterly claps,
erasers of thunder, parabolas
of memory. Chinese kites, high over cliffs
no one has yet fallen off,
are swooping birds that skim the sea of
childhood, then the "all-at-once I'm seventeen
and old enough to ride the fun park roller
coaster...." Abandon the past, all ye who
want to do anything of significance:
try the tunnel of love or wander through
the Victorian haunted house of gabled
intentions and dilapidated desire.
At this appalling hour, craving is
an unsteady invalid in a white
nightgown— a young Bette Davis, who descends
the curving staircase with a candle that pins
her indecisive shadow to the wall.
We in the audience pray- and even,
somehow, *know*- that when she falls, as she must,
she won't injure herself, she won't set
anyone's house of cards on fire—we *know*
she will establish herself as mistress
of the brief collapse, we *know* she will survive
another long stretch of cinematic
moments- she will make it to a gentle
decrescendo, not a Hollywood cheat, but
an ending we can all embrace as happy.

THE RECEPTION LINE

Last night, I dreamt about Aunt Percy,
the spunky alcoholic I so loved for
being who she was-- funny and flawed.
Leaving a bar one night when she was young,
she rammed her car into a back road bridge abutment,
then made her way in heels to the closest farm
and called the police, complaining that someone
had moved the bridge. Aunt Percy, old, was in
my dream's reception line: she offered apricots:
cold and sweet. "Aunt Percy," I said, you look
wonderful. "But thin," she said, and it wasn't good.
A question came up: someone in the family
needed immediate help. "Don't worry,"
I said, which is almost always a mistake.
I think dream-talking with the dead may be
a sign my own death's not far off, and
there's little time left for me to tell it
like I think it is, which is the farthest
honesty can take us while we breathe.
In the dream, I spoke to my father,
and was glad to see him looking well.
The last real time was in a Scottsdale hospital:
I went in as soon as the nurses were done
with bathing and shaving and feeding him.
Garbled as he was, he got out my name and
mumbled something about "feet" and "cold."
I rubbed his feet till he signaled me to stop,
left a picture of my mother by his bed,
and walked back to his nearby empty house,
meaning to return after lunch. I was
hardly in the door when the hospital called…
In the dream, my father, too, was standing in
the reception line: he looked happy and
healthy. I said I was glad to see him. Then,
I added, speaking from someplace deeper than
memory, "You're my father, among other things."
When I woke up, I knew: my father's love
was like a ship and the ship wrecked and
went down and wood floated to the shore of
the island of my life, and I picked up

all the timber I could and used it for
fires when the nights were cold.
When we die, it doesn't matter what we had,
only what we did. You may, like me,
be so close to the edge,
your feet are beginning to get cold.
Your dead, too, may have formed a reception line--
and so many in our family need immediate help.

SISTER MARY ALGEBRA

Sister Mary Algebra is trimming
integers. Buzzing Zeroes come skimming
across a bobbing sea of students who *know*,
and dive bomb us prisoners of the final row,

outfielders captive within the sweating walls
of a prison where a backward glance stalls
the ticking horse, and chalky soil turns seeds
of numbers to squadrons of rosary beads.

Beyond our lidded window, the hot day
wanders benches like a long-haired stray,
sticking its nose in filth and dog-eared glories,
panting like the nuns in our washroom stories

of sex. After lunch is Phys. Ed., last
niche in St. Jude's side: coaches aghast
at our losses describe with cracking lips
trajectories, while uncoiling paper clips.

Finally, they let us loose out where God's love
is the smack of bat on ball, ball on glove:
the music of spheres mounts in the score:
and we are the players the numbers are for.

OH say can you see The angels are people and people are falling Buildings are burning The towers have staggered and still the plane's coming It's coming it's coming The hard-wired jaws of Apocalypse open They open they open Oh, can you see? Zero planes coming Death numbers numbing Towers are tumbling Oh, say can you see Not God with dice But Apocalypse now It's now It's now The needle of now is stuck on the spinning Is stuck on the nightmare Is opening jaws so the skyway is falling This is hell and we're in it We're in it together The devil is faceless Oh, say can you see Can you face now the faceless A hole in the sky and the skyline keeps burning and people keep falling Stop planes in the rerun Run out in the street to stop people from falling Our smoke is in space Our whole world is burning No theme but terror the answer survival Everyone down in a whale that is burning Policemen and firemen friends who won't leave us and people on cell phones I'm dying I love you Do we know what has happened? This is evil triumphant, the face of the faceless its jaw wired open Oh say can you see any hole in this nightmare where people are running and blue sky is falling Oh say can you see anything but a nightmare of ashes and rubble and noise in the streets We fall on our knees like children who ask- No it's we who ask children- Kids, do you hear? the world has exploded the grownups have failed you Bang your cup Break your pencil Turn away from our lectures and all explanations Hold each other Remember Burn your guns Tear your clothing Sit alone by a river but the rivers are burning You're too scared to touch them Oh my god oh my god It's too late to forsake You It's too late to say No when the angels keep falling the towers keep burning a hole in the skyway The plane we're all on is a plane that's been hijacked We've lost our connection Our marble's on fire The death toll is mounting How high can you count them The rats in our houses are gnawing ice cream while the fire ball's burning Oh children are laden with nightmare and fire Oh say can you hear terror calling your name Your child on the cell phone and all of us dying We are the angels and all of us fallen Fallen and falling there's No Faith No Hope No God but One God a Love God a Circus God a God who will swallow our Daggers of Fire a God to Believe in who'll Believe us not Leave us or Nothing will Stay of us or our Children Our Children in Ashes Oh say can we Say Love can we See Love can we Be Love right now? If so Say and Pray for Tomorrow No more Terror No more Terror No More Terror No More

INHERITANCE

Grandfathers are always dying. Mine
had strokes in Florida, cancer of
the throat in Michigan. He tried to whine
but pipes in his neck like parts of a stove
turned his smallest whisper to a boom.
He scorned the striped pajamas he got as gifts,
complained about the loud curtains in his room.
He mocked doctors and nurses alike, and sniffed
suspiciously at us. He chuckled when
he made me cry. Up to the last, he harped
on all my faults, and tried his best to din
it into me that I was dumb. He carped
about my every move. And yet his dying
testament was that he'd always loved me most.

LOOK AT THE STARS
poem for a high school graduation

When I was a high school graduate, roughly three
hundred years ago, my father took me
to Paris. I don't remember the sights we
saw— the Louvre, the Eiffel Tower.
All I recall is one evening hour,
walking with dad on the Champs Elysees,
how he pointed up at the night sky to say
the one French sentence he sort of knew:
"Regardez les etoiles dans le ciel."

You've changed what you think, where you go, how you run,
when you speak, who you are in the public sun,
and you feel new *why's* when the night has burned
and turned to cinders the day's disguise.
You've learned much more than you realize yet,
more than the facts, most of which you'll forget,
more than the theories you'll need to unravel.
Sitting in classrooms, you learned to travel.

See <u>now</u>, and the obvious truth will come clear:
you're each a gift, it's amazing you're here…
But since there's no "other," no "them"— just "we,"
drown your demands in the depths of the sea
like pirated treasure in tangled kelp:
our world is in trouble; we need you to help.

My father's French sentence sounds silly, it's true,
but it's still the present I offer you:
"Regardez les etoiles," or try—
wherever you are, see the stars in the sky.
Observe the chill beauty of stellar space,
the cohorts of clarification above,
then warm to the beauty of our human place,
eyes you look into, looking back with love.

THE PATH FROM YOU TO GOD

YOU
wake from
a dream and
the dream is still hanging
you're an iceberg adrift in the
sea of yourself and the dream is
a drama but not in the ballpark of
meaning and message and changing and chance
it's reaching and stretching and pushing against the thick
glassy limit of the little you know and just when you think you
can see through the limit thought seizes like an engine it balks like
a horse and it throws you it throws you it throws you, you
fall and keep falling you fall until all goes settle or
smash and then you miraculous find you can
move and your legs lift your arms lift
they're wings and you are a seabird
high over water not falling
you're flying you're
calling crying
GaaKaaa
GOD

A PRAYER FOR AUTHORS
(revisionist homage to Ilya Kaminsky)

I walk the same blind surrender
over and over
Can I live? is a kind of petition.
I run on edge through rooms
holding the white furniture of prayer:
a cross, a poem, a flag…
I have to carry them
without asking
what dance this is.
To sleep, I have to
move in front of the mirror
and praise a language
in which music is a madness
that will not disturb us.
I want to wake up
I want to speak about the year I live, Lord,
the darkest music
of your actual streets,
the mine of my days
But who will I speak for?
myself? this dead animal, my body?
To speak what this is
I must leave the page
empty

A POEM THAT ESCAPED ME

Once there was an exile
inhabited by a man.

Once there was a fountain
thirsty for water

Once there was a death--

Who would you be
if you were alive?

It has been years
since she paid attention to the clock
since she visited herself
since she shivered under
rough blankets and ready touching

I'm not talking about
here a heart, there a heart
open the door, they're coming in the window
or a card game
or a tin song played with two fingers
over and over

I am trying to tell you
of a solitude so high
it keeps out rain

a burned organ
in a cathedral
so bombed it accepts
the blue inevitable

I am talking about
a black dog
children set fire to,
to watch it run through the town like
a hot stutter

there are bitternesses
to which one becomes addicted
there are barricades
one cannot storm

there are lives
you never get over

THE OX

This is an ox.
Look at the ox.
The ox does not look at you,
He is big and beautiful
You are skinny with freckles.
Your legs knock together when you run.
You are afraid of the ox.
He is behind a fence but your father needs to fix it.
The ox is not afraid of you.
But in a year or so, you will learn to yoke the ox.
You will ride the ox and one day you will help to kill the ox.
You will use his hide to warm your bed at night.
The ox is owned by a man in China who is old and rich.
You do not know the man in China exists.
In this, you are like the ox.
In not so many years, you will meet the man from China and marry
the man from China because your freckles will
have been bleached away and your stringy hair will
turn out to be long and glossy and black and your eyes will
be praised for their brightness and depth.
He will use you to warm his bed at night.
In this, you are like the ox.
You look at the ox.
The ox does not look at you.

GOODBYE, GODOT
    for Mohsen

This is a man who embraces snow.
He has the juice of pomegranates on his thumbs.
He and the snow are always disappearing.

Sparrows tremble on vines-
vines that are still there in the dust-
after the battle
after the war.

I'm not his mother, not his lover.
I have no culture. I had no war.
He is male, eastern, dark, young…
He is central to what I forget.
I am a memory he doesn't have.

We are each to the other
the ghost of an imaginary friend,
the breath in the wind.

What might have been a poem
is stained with blood in Tehran
and coffee in Seattle.

A Seattle waiter arrives at the table
his pocket says HELLO! MY NAME IS GODOT.
He bears a glass tray, a mirror--
round as a moon or a pomegranate:
the mirror falls-
the waiter's been shot—

waiter, fruit, and glass break open-
blood and seed and sweetness mix with glass shards.

With delicate fingers he separates
fruit from fragments.
He puts the mirror back together
in the shape of a stained glass outcry…
In the future, you might find him
lying at the heart of a Persian desert

in long improbable
American grass…

These are words from which
we've disappeared.

But no (meaning yes)
I love you
I'm here
a vine in the dust
after the war—

And any trembling sparrow
is welcome to light on me.

THINGS KEEP TAKING YOU AWAY FROM ME

your grandmother
sadness
rain

I refuse to embrace your absence

you open the window
and scatter like ash

you leave
no words behind

just your yellow umbrella
that green vine
this clear bottle

LIFE WITH ENRIQUE

Elementary School

Before I met you, I made fun of your name.
Enrique Rico, I called you.
In church, you were the valley between your sisters.

My parents made me have you over.
You rang the bell and stood on the stoop
in slacks that matched your jacket.
You spoke in a voice as chill as pudding.
When you sat, you kept your knees together.
My mother loved you.

You had a wooden train set
 the station taller than I was.
Your father made it himself.
Your trains came with stories,
 you'd just say the start:
"This train is called Ricky.
 He loves Amy for her bright red hair.
 Rickey feels sad.
 Amy feels nothing."

 I, whose hair was stiff as straw,
 wondered who Amy was.

You said, when asked,
 you never crawled beneath the covers
 to read by flashlight while others slept.
You said you lay awake
and stared out the window.
You said you never thought of me—
awake under the same stars,
five doors down the street....

I dreamed I was a train and
ran on a track
on a bed of invisible stones,
all of them
marked with my name.

When I woke up,
I wanted to be Amy-
flame lighting up her hair
and burning down her feelings.

Middle School

You never played our after-school games, Enrique.
One was Initiation.
We sat the newest kid
at the edge of someone's living room.
Then we took thin-stemmed glasses and constructed
a winding maze on the bare-wood floor.
We gave the kid a minute or two
to map out a route across the room.

Then someone took the person away
to blindfold in another room.

While they were gone,
we cleared the glasses
and someone led the person back.

The blinded person began the crossing.
Some shuffled or walked an invisible wire
winding a torturous way
across an empty floor.

Some teetered, some wavered
and flailed their hands,
trying to keep from breaking glass
while we called out
made up directions,
 pretend concern—
"No! No!"
"Watch out!"
"Go right!"
 One girl
 overweight
 eager to please
 lost her balance
 and crashed to the ground.…

Adulthood

When the blindfold came off
and you left me, Enrique,
I found myself lying
on our living room floor
in a sea
of invisible broken glass.

PARADELLE ON LOVE

Once, our hearts were open. We made love.
We made love once our hearts were open.
We turned and embraced in huge, unmade spaces ruined by war.
Unmade, we turned and embraced in huge spaces ruined by war.
Once we turned and embraced open war
in huge spaces we made, our hearts were ruined by unmade love.

Have you vanished from the face of this life?
You have vanished from the face of this life.
Still, I miss longing, and belonging to you to have love
I still miss longing to have love and belonging to you.
I have vanished from life to miss this longing,
and still you have the face of love belonging to you.

Our old blind pain did not help us find a way to God.
Our old pain did not help us find a way to blind God.
God could not let us be true to one another.
One God could not let us be true to another.
Let us find another blind God to be true to.
Our old one way pain God did not, could not help us.

Our blind way of belonging to old war
turned our hearts' spaces to pain. We once embraced love,
and could have vanished from another God,
to find the one true face to help us. You were not open,
God. You did not let be, and have ruined us. And still
in this unmade life made huge by longing, I miss love.

A CLEAR GLASS BOWL

*An open meadow, high in the mountains.
I sit cross-legged in a full skirt,
comfortable on the warm spring ground,
and there is suddenly a flower in my lap,
petal lapped on petal
white as a formal invitation,
in the sky-blue valley of my skirt.
And I lift the blossom to my face.
I breathe deeply of its sweet aroma--
the wild and eager fragrance
tells me of meadows
I have visited
only in my imagination.
Then I lift my eyes and see-
this kind of flower grows abundantly
in this high meadow;
I still hold it a miracle
this singular bloom has come to me,
brought by the breezes into my lap.
I arise in gratitude.
I take the blossom to my mountain home,
and float it in a clear glass bowl.
I smile at the flower in deep appreciation
of its form and fragrance.
I will be smiling
even when the flower is gone....*

*Even when I am gone,
I will be smiling.*

WILLIAM OF THE APPLES AND THE ARROW

The old way of pinning a word so it goes
on the line that stretches between the green
of the tree and the other is gone. They need
to be grouped, all the washcloths, all the wet
clothing like the faces of children who get
scared when they have to go in the building
they have to call home.. Home on the range, on.
the run, means hot, means children need to prepare.
Everything needs to be grouped like clothes by
size and shape and round or red or hung straight-
straight-leggéd like blue jeans hung up to dry.
Line up wet soldiers in rows and they'll try
to be ready for business, but beware
of the orders of socks and shoes they'll get
like secret sentences. It all shakes down to
someone's decision and whoever it was,
it wasn't me, it wasn't at all <u>this</u>-
this William, William of the apple and
spent arrows- William, the son in whom our
father found himself mostly disappointed
because this boy was somehow caught up short,
he was found out, this one, snagged or dragged here,
he was found somehow guilty, which is why,
I think, he was stripped of medals and
glasses and pockets to put them in.
So if I wonder or taste ashes and
echoes of closets or classes, I still sit
shackled, unable to find things to speak of.
I have lost more than I can name- And
this thing where I am seated does not have
wheels which go round and round as we sang
assembled, they go hot against my hands
as I force them them forward, make them take me
as a citizen, and when the circle's squared,
I find myself here, back in a room they say
is mine though this is the first I've seen it,
with a person, you, a girl with a smile
like clothing on a line, flapping in the wind-
saying we are related, saying you know me.

RODIN'S GIRLFRIEND

Welcome to Montdevergues, asylum for
the crazy and the inconvenient. Why,
I wonder, have you come exactly now,
November 19th, 1917?
I've had visitors before, but one or two,
not <u>several</u>. Never mind. I'm prepared
to talk about what used to be my life.
Once upon a time, I was Camille Claudel,
young and beautiful and gifted. I am
fifty three now, and as you see me…
The first time I saw Rodin, I was nineteen,
and thought intelligence led to happiness.
Rodin had devised a word test to
discover what he called "sculptural promise."
He asked me to say two nouns quickly, without
thinking. I answered, and he took me as his
student then and there. Much later when we
first made love, he told me future sculptors
favored an abstract/human combination:
I had answered *maiden* and *death*. So then
I asked, "But of those two, *death* and *maiden*,
which is <u>human</u>, which <u>abstract</u>?" Now, here I am,
an ancient maiden. And here you are.
You came to tell me what I already know—
Rodin is dead. Long live Rodin. Despite
all that happened, I would grieve for him,
cast myself headlong into mourning here, in
front of you, but we dead are not famous for
emotional displays. Death messengers, you
were like years ago me, hastening through
Paris streets, trying not to bleed and bleeding,
arriving at the studio, finding him
alone. Imagining his hands on my breasts
like milking spiders, I said— "Auguste,
I lost the baby. I was squatting
to relieve myself when it dropped out, down
into the Paris sewer. I heard it
cry out when it landed in the moving muck."
"Ah, you took something," he said, and a smile
  slashed the bottom of his face. "Poor Camille.

It must have been dreadful. You must have thought
life as we know it was coming to an end."
He didn't understand: life as we know it
is *always* coming to an end. I hated
his smile, I hated his gratitude. He was
grateful because he thought me guilty of
the murder of our child.... I am exhausted.
Let me close, please, with a benediction
"Imaginary God, tormented and
 tormenting in the name of love—have
 mercy on our souls, so human, so abstract."

A WOMAN OF YEMEN

She has walked with the women of her village-
to the well and halfway back,
more fluid than the water she has carried
pillowed on her head in a plastic jug.
Her clothes are fluid on her fluid body,
a scarf wound around her head,
flowing down her back in rivulets,
a cotton dress with hanging sleeves,
fabric stiff and soft against her skin.
She refuses to observe her observation,
turning away from the camera before
it can fasten on her, swiveling away
from the woman who the women say
comes from America,
the woman they say is thirty-nine
and still unmarried
so her students pray for her,
the students she teaches a foreign language.
The other women pray for <u>her</u>, as well,
to be safe, to be charitable.
But she does not pray for the American or herself,
because she has learned that prayers don't work.
She looks and listens,
perched on the edge of her yellow jug,
half on, half off—
half in a place where there are no jugs or villages,
no meals to cook or mouths to feed
because the greatest freedom is freedom from the thought
there is more that needs doing.
She wanders freely within her mind,
looking at the rocks and the green
spilling over them,
waiting for something she cannot imagine,
something to surprise her with a new fluidity
of breeze or being-
knowing sometimes there are graces in the green
which only the observant see.

She enjoys the breeze
flowing down for a moment from the hills.
And the American woman
feels in her, in the stance she assumes,
half sitting, half leaning, a sisterhood
she can only express through an image
she hopes will capture the other in a moment.
So the moment becomes an image, and the image
becomes ours, becomes one of sisterhood, of common *being*,
in which all who look and try to learn
are necessarily included.

A MAN OF YEMEN

This man
uses his knife-
clean, sharp-
to make fine distinctions.

Analyzer of
animals,
he separates
with surgical precision
flesh from bone,
meat from fat.

This man is fastidious-
dedicated to
the practice of an ancient art,
a meticulous religion.

His life's work
divides a red sea-
this used one way
this, another.

Everything is wanted.
Nothing is wasted.

This man
is not
an American butcher.

she moves swiftly

down the narrow street/ moves toward the man there/ the one she's been seeking for thirty-five years/ since he backed away at the last from her parents/ not saying the words that had to be said/ she wears the shawl he gave her at first/ she remembers the way he held it out without looking/ held it out in both hands/ in hands that were shaking/ she thinks she can see/ in the man just ahead/ the slope of his shoulders, the curve of his neck/ it's been thirty-five years but she knows she will know him/ by the look in his eyes/ having seen in his young face/ how the old man would be/ as she sees in the mirror/ the young girl she was/ she knew when she took/ the shawl from his hands/ when she felt it lying across her own/ when she said "I am honored" as they told her to do/ she could feel the truth of her/ sudden impossible feeling for him/ filling the formal pronouncement/ like wine in a goblet and she knew/ she had given herself to him/ just like that, all at once/ a gift that could not be ungiven/ and though she expects when she reaches/ the light where the street ends/ when she sees the face of the man who is there/ and he's no one she knows/ her girlish dream will turn into ash/ still she keeps moving/ the heart in her chest/ going side to side/ like a rag doll shaken in the mouth of a dog/ and in spite of what happens or fails to/ when she reaches the light at the end of the street/ she would not give up/ this heart-racking moment/ for all that is real and solid in the bricked up world

EDGE POEM

Is love a sustainable passion, a shared solitude, or
a web for learning new ways to fail? Yes. Sky through the door-
way is just a high place to fall from, but a delicate girl
is dangerous. Holding a pomegranate like a grenade, she'll
wake you up to who you are. Your love for her will cost you
everything. I don't think you need to know more than that. Too
much knowing changes the outcome of event: it's an old way of
pulling things apart- tearing the fabric so you go from place to
place without getting anywhere- and feeling is a form of
non-linear progression, a fact-finding trip to a place where
no one can live. But if you name what isn't there, you possess
it like a bee owns honeycomb, or a rabbi owns the Talmud,
and all there is to see or say is a gift. Writers sustain their
passion by writing, readers read to share their solitude. Oh, Yes.

NED'S ARIA

Beginnings, yes. But who knows how things will end?
As a feverish child, singing in my everyday sickbed,
I didn't. Neither did my seamstress mother, forced to bend
every night over her own lap, biting off thread
as she sewed. She said, "The truth isn't in wine,
or song. If you want the truth, you have to divine

it like underground water, with a stick, not try to define
it as yours, but the one truth worth knowing, we learn at the end."
My Sunday school teachers didn't confine
themselves to the truth: "Sing at the table, sing in bed,"
they told me. "The Devil will get you when you're dead."
They really thought-- I thought, as well-- God would send

singers of love songs to hell. But my path there took a sudden bend
in high school, when my art teacher praised "the Romantic, divine
Fragonard..." She said Classicism was hanging by a thread,
his swinging girl, her half-off shoe, marked its end.
I hung a poster of that girl above my bed:
I could almost hear her singing. Some nights, I'd dream her fine

blue day, her lover, her after-world, were mine--
I'd swing into heaven on a song! But that dream would end
in daylight guilt, my covers at the foot of my bed…
Mom said "You need dates, Carolyn— a cocktail party line."
Her words wandered. When she finally found the deep end
of her life, her mind bent over, and bit off the thread

of her thought. Ned, my college voice coach said
"Your voice is hopeless, and I love you." Ned drank too much wine,
but he wove my name into an aria. He became my friend,
my confidante, my lover. The school year came to an end,
and Ned had no job. He got drunk and enlisted one fine
May day— Nine months later, his last letter home said

"Music obscures the truth."   When I'm lying in bed
  some nights, the aria Ned rewrote for me starts to thread
  its way through the dark of my mind like a musical vine.
  The ticking clock is a metronome, then, not a mine.
  I hear his love song coming from beyond the bend,
"Car-o-lyn ben, Cre-di-mi al-men."

  A sword hangs by a thread above the bed
  I call mine. I hope our spirits will blend into mercy
  like music at the end: it's a hope I savor like wine.

RECRUDESCENCE

I started as a hoofer on a farm
in Kansas, two hundred pounds of hog.
I remember white-washed wooden troughs, warm
buckets of kitchen scraps coming down the hill
at dusk, the tractor grinding gears, the chain saw
whining. I remember standing perfectly still,
flank to flank with my fellows, whenever the dog
barked a certain way. At the packing plant, they
cut off my head, skinned me, cleaned me—the next day
they reduced me to chops. At the A & P,
they gave me parsley sprigs, a styrofoam bed,
plastic wrap. A housewife in jeans said
I looked good. She brought me home and froze me.
Minutes ago, she took me out, put me on
this china plate, left me to lie in the sun.
Already I feel a nervous chain
Reaction—almost pleasant, or not quite pain.
I am softer, warmer—I will soon be raw.

PROTEST POEM

steady white cow
alone with her nine stomachs
milling green in a field paved with shadows
her sudden singularity
freeze-frames unconcern:
seen sidelong, she's a
handkerchief pinned
to the line, wind-stiff,
an unutterable promise
of milk to be delivered,
white as a white box,
as a white boat,
as a freshly-painted
white door
on a white barn,
she is undeniable --
nothing you say
can make her other
than what she is -
a four-footed fact, she stands,
and thus she refutes you:
<u>Mu</u>.

ROXANNE'S ROOM

It's the 50s. I'm eleven. I'm in Roxanne's room.
There's a blue phonograph by a westward-facing window.
It's late autumn, late afternoon, the sun is shining.
Roxanne puts on a record.
I hear castanets, a guitar,
the sounds of someplace far away,
where I have never been.
Out of a blur of sound comes a trumpet, rising
in defiance of my little life.
In 1966, I buy my first record.
Miles Davis, Sketches of Spain.
When I play it, out come castanets, a guitar,
the sounds of someplace far away,
where I have never been.
Out of a blur of sound comes a trumpet, rising
in celebration of my little life.
I'm seventy. I have cancer. I'm dying.
I put on "*Concierto de Aranjuez*,"
and it's the 50s. I'm eleven.
I'm in Roxanne's room
listening to her blue phonograph.
I hear castanets, a guitar,
the sounds of someplace far away,
a place where I am going.
It's late autumn, late afternoon, the sun is shining.

ABOUT THE AUTHOR

Lyn Coffin is the author of more than thirty books— poetry, fiction, and drama. She has translated writers from Farsi (Mohsen Emadi), Georgian (Shota Rustaveli) and Czech (Jiri Orten). She has been the recipient of several grants and awards, including The Saba Prize in 2016. One of her short fictions was in the Best American Short Stories edited by Joyce Carol Oates. Her book of Seifert translations, *The Plague Monument*, was used by the Nobel Committee in granting Seifert his prize. Her plays have been performed internationally (Sweden, Malaysia) and in many US cities (off-off Broadway New York, Detroit, Boston, Seattle). This year will see the publication of her novel, *The Aftermath*, and a children's book, *Henry & Punkin* (illustrated by Reza Bigonah), both published by IronTwine Press, and a book of her poetry and that of Mercedes Luna Fuentes, entitled *Rifles & Reception Lines*, in a bilingual edition published by Whale Road Books. Her work has been translated into Egyptian, Spanish, Czech, Farsi, Georgian, Swedish, Mongolian, Russian, French and German.

ABOUT THE COVER ARTIST

Maria Tarasoff is a professional artist who travels the world capturing subtle details of place and culture. She graduated with a BFA (photography major) in 2003 and has exhibited within Canada and internationally. She currently works with the Canadian design company Farmboy Fine Arts producing imagery for hotels such as Marriott, Wyndham, and Hilton. Her photos are in hotels from Abu Dhabi to the Bahamas, Miami to Doha. In 2009 she embarked on a year long residency in Sana'a, Yemen which produced a extensive collection of pre-Arab Spring imagery and sparked a love of the Yemeni landscape and culture. She currently lives in Kamloops BC but spends most of her time abroad.